# SELF-DEFENSE:
## A STUDENT GUIDE TO WRITING POSITION PAPERS

### Kevin Possin

*Philosophy Department*
*Winona State University*

## The Critical Thinking Lab

Library of Congress Control Number: 2001119630


ISBN: 0-9712355-2-X




Published by

**The Critical Thinking Lab**
**Pleasant Valley Road**
**RR3 Box 83B**
**Winona, MN 55987**

*Let's face it, writing is hell.*
William Styron


*Writing is an exploration. You start from
nothing and learn as you go.*
E.L. Doctorow


*Writing is the act of burning through
the fog in your mind.*
Natalie Goldberg


*I write to understand
as much as to be understood.*
Elie Wiesel


*How do I know what I think
until I see what I say?*
E.M. Forester


*The mere process of writing is one of the
most powerful tools we have for
clarifying our own thinking.*
James Van Allen

# Table of Contents

## Introduction

So you have to write a position paper. Well, the first thing to realize is this: It's not as bad as it may seem. It's not like you're having root canal work or something. In fact, if you follow the recipe and suggestions discussed in this manual, writing a position paper will be relatively painless and maybe even enjoyable. And, if you're not careful, you'll probably learn something—about your topic, about writing, about critical thinking, and about yourself—about your own beliefs and values.

A position paper is just critical thinking, written down.

Writing position papers is different from writing reports, take-home exams, letters, or stories—so different that, while you might be good at the latter, you might suck at the former. It's not as if one has a natural knack for writing position papers [I sure didn't!]. It takes practice—for everyone. But this manual will definitely help [or I wouldn't have busted my hump writing it!].

## The 4 basic ingredients

When you omit one of the basic ingredients of an apple pie, you end up with *something*, but it won't be an apple pie. If you omit the crust, you get apple sauce or crisp. If you omit the apples and substitute Ritz crackers, you get "mock" apple pie (or at least that's what the folks at Ritz say you get; I'd have another name for it ;-) Similarly with an effective position paper.

An effective position paper has at least four basic ingredients:

1

1. Statement of position
2. Arguments for position
3. Reconstruction of alternative positions
4. Critical review of alternative positions

If your paper consists of only the first ingredient, it's not even a position paper. It's a position statement. Corporations, for example, issue these periodically, just to let stockholders, etc., know what a company's policy is on an issue.

If your paper consists of only the first two ingredients on this list, it's a position paper, but a very ineffectual one. Your reader will be inclined to think, "Well, you've got your position and even arguments for it, but I've got *my* position and arguments for it too. So there!" At most you've reached a stalemate in the eyes of this reader, and you don't want to settle for that. You want to show your readers **why you're so right** and **why they're so wrong**. You need all four ingredients in order to do this.

If your paper consists of only the last two ingredients on the list above, it's not a position paper at all either. It's a *critical review* of alternative positions on an issue, but it advances and argues for no position on that issue.

An effective position paper must have all four ingredients so that, in essence, you are saying to your reader, "Here's my position on this issue; here are my reasons for thinking my position is true; here are some alternative positions people often take on this issue, but here's why those positions are mistaken."

Now that you have an overview of these basic ingredients, let's look at each ingredient separately and in more detail.

## Statement of position

There are few things more irritating than being two pages into someone's paper or article and still wondering what the author's %@#! point is. Being obscure or roundabout is often used as a sign of being intellectual [even by too many professors]. But it's usually a sign of woolly-mindedness, lack of confidence, or lack of anything worthwhile and defensible to say. Most often, being un-clear about your position doesn't intrigue your reader; it just pisses them off.

Begin your paper, then, with a clear statement of your position; for example, "In this paper I will defend the position that some of the campaign ads for George Bush in the 1988 presidential election were racist." Cut right to the chase: "In this piece I will argue that Desert Storm was indefensible under Just War Theory and that this is so much the worse for Just War Theory." After reading either of these lead sentences, there is simply no room for your reader to ask, "I wonder what this paper is about?" unless they're brain dead.

You might preface your statement of position with a bit of stage setting that helps establish the importance of the topic or issue you are addressing, thereby motivating your reader to take an interest. For example: "It would be a tragedy for our democracy if a president were elected as a result of pandering to the racial prejudices of the electorate, and yet this could well have happened in the 1988 election." But be very careful with this kind of preface to your statement of position. Avoid "journalistic hooks"; for example, "As I munched my popcorn in front of the tube, the face of Willie Horton leered at me, and I wondered, 'Is this an ad for the latest horror movie or is this an election year?'" A cutesy intro like this just undercuts your credibility. [And the fact that many journalists write this way takes nothing away from my point!]

Also, don't write a bunch of lofty sounding dribble. For example, if you are writing a position paper on the legal voting age, don't begin with, "The age at which citizens should acquire the right to vote has baffled mankind since Plato, the Father of Philosophy, wrote the masterful treatise on political theory, *The Republic.*" This kind of fluff is often patently false or at least so vacuous and pompous that your reader's eyes have rolled back so far they're in their proper position again.

You don't want to gag your reader; you simply want to get them to see the relevance of the issue you're addressing. And this can be done in a simple sentence or two. Often citing a poll that indicates people's interest in your topic is an effective way of doing this. Essentially, you should answer the efficient reader who is asking, "Why should anyone give a damn about this issue anyway?"

Often there is no need to motivate readers' interest, for instance, if your paper is on such "hot button" topics as abortion, welfare, censorship, or monumental Supreme Court decisions. When this is the case, skip the intro and launch right into the statement of your position.

Properly "flag" your position when you state it; for example, "The position I will defend in this paper is...." Make things as easy for your reader to follow as possible. Pointing things out to your reader like this might seem a bit dry by way of a writing style, but keep in mind that one of your primary goals when writing a position paper is clarity.

Lastly, make sure you really are taking a position on the issue you're addressing. A position is a claim that something is true or right or that something is false or wrong, for example, that human cloning is too dangerous to be ethically acceptable or that making environmental protection laws more stringent will increase rather than decrease jobs. Discussing how people are divided on such issues is not a position paper—it's just a *report* on people's positions. To take a position you must go out on a limb and hazard an answer on an issue. Don't hedge; stake out your claim!

Incidentally, to think that there is *no* defensible position on an issue *is itself a position*—one that probably requires more argumentation than taking a traditional stand. For to defend this position would require that you argue that *all* the arguments for *all* the more traditional positions are faulty. Talk about a load of work!

Furthermore, to think that *any and all* positions on an issue are *equally* defensible is itself a singular position, one that also probably requires more argumentation than taking a traditional stand. For to defend this position would require that you argue that *all* the arguments for *all* the traditional positions are equally successful or that the issue in question is just a matter of taste, like whether strawberries taste good, for instance. Talk about a load of work again!

Only rarely is it the case that all positions on an issue are equally defensible or indefensible. So if you are inclined to think that all opinions on an issue are of equal value, ask yourself if you have *thoroughly* investigated the issue. Remember, usually the best explanation for the diversity of opinion is ignorance, not the equality of opinion—witness the diversity of theories throughout the history of science.

## Arguments for your position

After you have explicitly stated your position, you have the task of justifying it by means of arguments. You must give the reader reasons for thinking that your position on the issue is true or correct, such that they too should believe or adopt it. Anyone can have an opinion, but unless you have good reasons for thinking it's true, you're irrational for adopting it, and others need not give you the time of day for just making a mere assertion of it.

As you lay out your arguments for your position, flag them accordingly so as to make your paper reader friendly. For example, introduce your first argument with, "My first argument for this position is the following." [Flag subsequent arguments with the likes of, "Another reason for thinking..., is that...."]

### *Give complete arguments*

As you give your arguments, be complete and detailed enough so that someone who knows nothing about the issue could read your paper and understand how it is that your arguments work as reasons for believing your position. *Imagine that your reader is someone who is not in the class.* Envisioning your instructor as your audience only tempts you to *allude* to arguments rather than to *give* them; for example, "My first reason for thinking that workfare will not be an effective means of welfare reform is the bureaucratic problems with it that we discussed in class." And which problems are they!! You can't merely *mention* arguments, you have to *use* them to defend your position.

When you give an argument for your position, you are essentially answering the reader who asks, "Why should I believe your position?" After you have answered this question by means of your argument, however, it might be perfectly appropriate for the reader to ask a follow-up question regarding what you've just written: "OK, but why should I believe *that*?" For example, say that you are taking the position that the government ought to censor violent pornography, and say you have argued for this by claiming that such pornography causes a significant number of sexual assaults by inducing viewers to enact violent scenes they find in that pornography. If you leave things at that, however, in all likelihood your reader will simply wonder what reasons there are for believing *this*.

You must provide another argument in support of your first one. You have to provide a reason for thinking that your reason for thinking that certain forms of pornography are justifiably censored *is a good reason*. [Yes, that last sentence *is* correct.] For example, you could detail some of the psychological research done on the behavioral effects of viewing violent pornography. My point is that, if your argument for your position is just as controversial as your position is, you must argue in support of that argument. If you can't, then you'd better go hunting for a better, more self-sufficient, argument.

If, after reading the last paragraph, you are beginning to think that this process of giving an argument for one's argument could go on indefinitely, you don't have to worry about this. First, keep your audience in mind—what basic assumptions would they likely grant you? You may then use these assumptions as a starting point for your arguments. Second, and more generally, you are finished giving back-up support for your arguments when you honestly can no longer make sense of a reader sincerely asking why they should believe that the reasons you have provided are effective. While this is no guarantee that those reasons you've provided *are* effective, it does guarantee that you have made an intellectually honest effort to give a complete argument for your position. And that's the most and the least of your duties here.

### *How many arguments?*

By now you're probably asking, "How many different arguments should I give in defense of my position?" Theoretically, all you need is one, but it had better be a conclusive one that makes your position a dead certainty. The problem with this, however, is knowing whether or not your argument is that strong. Would you bet your life on a single horse? It would be OK, if you *knew* the horse was a sure winner, but that is seldom the case.

Same with arguments. Don't risk having your whole case ride on a single argument, if you don't have to. Use multiple arguments; distribute the weight of your case; and err on the side of overkill in defense of your position. That way, if one argument fizzles on you, you've got another one or two in reserve. On the other hand, don't wear your reader out by throwing *too* many arguments at them. With this shotgun approach, you also end up looking desperate. Pick the best batch of arguments; your ability to select better arguments will improve with practice.

### *What makes an argument good?*

What constitutes a *good* argument for a position is a huge topic—covered, by the way, in my *Critical Thinking* etext and software ;-) All I can do at this point is discuss a couple requirements for a good or "cogent" argument.

First, make sure the premises of your argument—that is to say the reasons you give for believing your position—are as believable as your position is, if not more so. For example, if you were to argue for the existence of God by appealing to the existence of miracles, you would be failing this first requirement, since it is highly controversial whether miracles exist. On the other hand, if you could argue for the existence of God by appealing to the existence of *people*, you would meet this requirement, since it's obvious that people exist.

Second, make sure the set of premises of your argument supports your position. That is to say, the truth of those premises must make your position probably true or at least more reasonable to believe than not. For instance, if you were to defend the moral permissibility of abortion by appealing to the fact that the majority of the population thinks it is morally acceptable, you would be failing this second requirement for a cogent argument, since popularity is no indication of truth.

So, if you find that a reason you are offering (for believing your position) fails either of these requirements—if it is at least as controversial as your position is or fails to make your position more reasonable to believe than not believe —you need to go hunting for a better argument for your position. Intellectual honesty demands it.

### Don't appeal to the dictionary

Say that you want to defend the moral permissibility of the death penalty. What would be wrong with using the following argument?

> *The American Heritage Dictionary* defines
> murder as "The unlawful killing of one
> human being by another, especially with
> malice aforethought." And State executions
> are neither unlawful, nor are they done with
> malice aforethought.

If this argument sounds too easy, *it is*. The dictionary is just a description of general linguistic practices. It is not an arbiter of, for example, morality. It tells us how we generally use the language, but it tells us little about *the nature of the world* we describe *by means* of language. So avoid this misuse of the dictionary. It is not a source of arguments for positions; in fact, many of its definitions are in sorry *need* of arguments.


### Address critics of your arguments

Earlier we discussed what measures you might have to take in order to give complete arguments, namely, giving reasons in support of your reasons for believing your position. In a similar vein, you might also have to support your argument by addressing a *critic* of it. This task arises when you use an argument that you know has flaws in its ability to support your position. Just as you would never knowingly use a leaky boat to row to your destination, without first patching the leak, so too you should never use a leaky argument to get to your conclusion, without first fixing the argument. So, when your argument is on record as having problems, intellectual honesty demands that you do one of two things: 1) dump the argument and find another with no known problems or 2) criticize your critic's argument against your argument.

Exercising this second option may look complicated, but it's easily managed. An example will illustrate what I'm talking about. Say that you are defending the position that abortion is morally permissible, and you have just supported that position by arguing that only living beings with certain cognitive capacities have rights; so the fetus does not have rights, for lack of those capacities. At this point it would be appropriate to fess up to a standard objection to this line of argument by saying, for example, "Now someone might very well criticize this argument by pointing out that people suffering severe brain damage also lack the relevant cognitive capacities in question, and yet it would be wrong to kill those patients without knowing that that is what they would have wished."

Once this criticism has been adequately detailed, it can be addressed in the following manner.

> This criticism of my argument is, however, ineffectual, since it is by no means clear that it *would* be wrong to remove from life-support human beings known to have no cognitive capacities due to severe brain damage. Such brain-damaged patients relevant to this discussion have *fewer* cognitive capacities than the typical guppy, and certainly the guppy has no status as a rightsholder. The moral qualms about removing life-support in cases of brain death result from confusing how one may treat a patient in their current cognitively incapacitated state with how one ought to have treated them when they were still a person—*prior* to their state of total cognitive incapacity.

Once the criticism of your argument has been disarmed, your argument is free once more to support your position.

Note in the example above how flags were used to tell the reader when the author is reconstructing the criticism and when they are criticizing that criticism.

BTW: If you have successfully criticized a criticism of your argument and then discovered a criticism of your criticism, intellectual honesty demands that you fess up to it and criticize it. Things are getting way complicated at this point, however. If you patch a boat, only to find that you must patch your patch, you might do well to consider getting a new boat! Similarly, if your argument needs this much maintenance, it may not be worth using; you might do better by using a different argument.

If you have, for example, three arguments for your position and all three arguments have criticisms that you are aware of, you must go through the above-discussed process three times. Address a criticism of your argument immediately after giving that argument. Don't rattle off all your arguments and then rattle off all their criticisms and then rattle off all your attempts to meet them. This only leads to confusion, as you force your reader to flip pages back and forth trying to figure out which criticism applies to which argument and which of your criticisms applies to which of your critic's criticisms.

### *Anticipating critics*

There are two other important ways of addressing your critics. These are more optional elements in a position paper, but they are often quite crucial for clarifying your arguments and defending your position from attacks.

For every position, there are good and bad arguments in defense of it. You want to use only good arguments. But you may also want to explicitly disassociate yourself from some of the bad arguments, so that your readers don't mistakenly ascribe them to you. To do this, tell your reader that you object to certain popular arguments for your position, reconstruct those arguments, and then criticize them. By doing this, you are sort of saying, "No, no, that's not me; that's my ne're-do-well brother."

If your topic is the least bit controversial, chances are a major portion of your audience will be predisposed to think your position is false. And they may have some reasons for thinking so. If you are aware of this, take the opportunity to reconstruct those criticisms of your position. Detail them as best as you can, and then give criticisms of those criticisms of your position. You want to give your critics their best shot at you and then show that even their best is not reason enough for thinking that your position is false. This is one major way to demonstrate the strength of your position—its ability to withstand criticism. Remember: Your job is show that your position has *the best arguments and the fewest problems.*

These optional elements can get a bit complicated, but if you flag things appropriately, there should be no problem. [I feel a mantra coming on: "If you flag them, they will follow."] For example, after you are done arguing for your position, you might kick things off by saying, "Someone may well object to my position by arguing as follows." After reconstructing the criticism, you can lead into your response to it by saying, "As persuasive as this criticism may sound, it has the following problem, however." Remember, help yourself to paragraph breaks for each of these parts.

13

## How your paper looks so far

Schematically, your paper so far should consist of the following basic elements:

1. Introductory statement as to the relevance of the issue
2. Statement of position
3. Argument for position
4. Reconstruction of criticism of argument
5. Criticism of criticism of argument
6. Reconstruction of criticism of position
7. Criticism of criticism of position

Some of these elements are omitted or repeated as appropriate. Element #1, for example, is omitted when the relevance or importance of the issue is obvious. Element #3 is repeated for every argument you give for your position. Elements #4-5 are omitted when, to the best of your knowledge, there is no criticism of the argument you used. Elements #4-5 are repeated for every criticism of your arguments. And Elements #6-7 are omitted when, to the best of your knowledge, there are no criticisms of your position; they are repeated for every such criticism you are aware of.

Each of these elements warrants its own paragraph. Paragraph breaks are free, so help yourself and help your reader.

And don't forget those flags, so the reader is never asking, "*Now* what's the author up to?"

Each of these elements is an answer to a question that you can use to focus your efforts while drafting your paper:

1. Why is the issue important in the first place?
2. What is my position on this issue?
3. What are my reasons or arguments for thinking my position is correct?
4. Are there any criticisms of my arguments?  If so, what are they?
5. Are there any criticisms of these criticisms?  If so, what are they?  If not, what other, criticism-free arguments are there for my position?
6. Are there any criticisms of my position?  If so, what are they?
7. Are there any criticisms of these criticisms?  If so, what are they?  If not, what other, criticism-free position is there?

And now, you're half done!

## Reconstruction of alternative positions

If you have picked an important issue on which to defend a position, chances are nearly certain that you are not the only one to have staked out a position on it.  So your reader is likely to be thinking, "Well, *you've* got good reasons for believing your position, but then *I've* got good reasons for believing *mine*, so it's a draw at best."  The second half of your position paper is devoted to settling this draw in favor of *your* position.

Your next job, then, is to find your most popular and your most worthy opponents.  By addressing the most popular alternative position, you are talking directly to the largest portion of your audience.  By addressing the strongest alternative position, you are demonstrating your intellectual honesty and willingness to put your position to the test. Once you have selected your alternative positions, reconstruct one, along with its arguments. [BTW: There might be only one alternative position; for example, either assassination *is* a morally justifiable military option or it is *not*.]

Properly flag your reconstruction; for example, "Not everyone agrees with me that the North American Free Trade Agreement with Mexico and Canada has hurt the U.S. job market. Some are of the opinion that the Agreement has actually helped the U.S. job market, by means of reaping cheaper products and creating more jobs in the import-export sector of the economy than were lost in the manufacturing sector."

Your reconstruction of your opponents should be done honestly, completely, and clearly. Avoid using "loaded language" as you detail your opponents' positions. For instance, if you have argued against gun control, don't reconstruct your opponent by saying, "There are some whiners who would render us helpless in defending ourselves against criminals by stealing our constitutionally protected firearms." [This just begs the question against your opponent, and we'll get to what that is in a minute.]

If you can do a better job of presenting the alternative positions and their arguments than their original authors have, you should do so. You wish to discuss only the worthiest, most compelling opponents in your paper, because, by defeating your strongest opponents, all the weaker ones fall automatically.

Yet another reason for examining the best alternative positions is perfectly captured by John Stuart Mill, in his essay *On Liberty* : "He who knows only his own side of the case knows little of that."

Incidentally, if you have defended a middle-of-the-road position, your opponents' positions will be found in both directions on the spectrum of possible positions on the issue you're addressing. To anticipate more readers' alternative positions, then, reconstruct positions from both ends of that spectrum. This will maximize the relevance and persuasiveness of your paper. For example, if you have argued that current restrictions on abortion (as they are limited in *Roe v. Wade*) are morally justified, then reconstruct a position (and accompanying arguments) that claims that *more* restrictions on abortion are justified and also reconstruct a position (and accompanying arguments) that claims that *fewer* such restrictions are justified.

**Critical review of alternative positions**

After you have reconstructed an alternative position and the main argument(s) for it, it's time to critically review either one or the other or (preferably) both. Note the difference between *criticizing an alternative position* and *criticizing an argument* for that alternative position. A successful criticism of an alternative position is an argument or reason for thinking that the position is false. On the other hand, a successful criticism of an argument for the alternative position simply nullifies that argument as a reason for thinking the alternative position is true. It's certainly better to give your opponent a reason for thinking their position is false—better than leaving your opponent with simply no reason for thinking their position is true. But the best you can do is both.

An example will bring this all into the clear. Say you have argued for the position that surrogate motherhood is perfectly morally permissible and that state restrictions on such a practice are not justified, because it is like any other contract for services rendered, just like hiring someone to paint one's house, for example. Now you are ready to critically review alternative positions in the following way.

Not everyone, however, shares this view of surrogate motherhood. Others believe that state restrictions of various degrees should be placed on this practice.

For example, one stand taken on surrogate motherhood is that it should be totally prohibited, because it is exploitative of lower-income women, in light of the modest fee received by the surrogate mother and the fact that virtually only women who are in desperate need of income are thereby interested in being surrogate mothers.

This argument, however, presupposes a very broad construal of exploitation, as simply giving someone in need an agreed upon modest income in exchange for a service. But it is highly questionable that this is morally objectionable, in view of the alternative in this case—viz., simply leaving the woman in her state of financial need. Admittedly, the income she in all likelihood receives for being a surrogate mother is modest, but so would it be if she were to seek employment many places elsewhere, e.g., at McDonald's—employment that can hardly be construed as morally objectionable enough to prohibit.

Furthermore, to prohibit surrogate motherhood is *itself* problematic, inasmuch as it removes an opportunity to receive an income for a capacity or skill the woman has—an opportunity to be self-sufficient and see to her own needs.

Another position taken on surrogate motherhood is that lesser restrictions should be placed on the contract between the "parents" and the surrogate mother, viz., that the latter should always have the option of returning the fee and keeping the child, at least until the child has been received by the "parents." The argument given for requiring this escape clause in the contract is that the surrogate mother often becomes emotionally attached to the fetus she carries, and to force her to relinquish the child upon its birth can be very traumatic for her.

This argument, however, is not a very compelling reason for requiring such an escape clause and giving the surrogate mother the right to exercise it. Admittedly, the surrogate mother often becomes emotionally attached to the child she bears, but then so too are many people with respect to their homes. They often find it a traumatic loss to have sold their homes. And yet it would be absurd to require that there be an escape clause in transfers of deed, which would allow the seller to return the downpayment (and whatever principle has been paid by the buyer) and demand the return of the house. Just as the party selling their home, only later to regret it, made a risky investment and has no right to expect others to cushion that risk, so too the surrogate mother makes a risky emotional investment and should not expect the "parents" to take the full brunt of cushioning it.

Note also that the buyer, if forced to take back the money and relinquish the house, would incur the loss of time and effort in their search for a home, not to mention *their* emotional investment in the house. The losses are similar for the "parents" in a surrogate motherhood arrangement, if, as this alternative position would have it, the arrangement can be broken on demand by the surrogate mother. The "parents" incur the loss of time and effort in their search for a child, not to mention the loss of *their* emotional investment in the child. And the surrogate mother seldom has any means of compensating them for these losses.

Notice how two alternative positions, along with their arguments, were reconstructed in the example above. Each position (with accompanying argument) warranted a separate paragraph. And each position (with accompanying argument) was immediately followed by its critical review, first of the argument for the position and then of the position itself. And each critical review warranted a separate paragraph.

Notice also how introductory flags were used in the example to tell the reader exactly what is being discussed —alternative position, argument for it, criticism of argument, and criticism of position.

### What makes a criticism good?

This is another huge topic, which I address much more extensively in my *Critical Thinking* etext. (Yes, this is another shameless plug ;-) But I can say this much here anyway: Criticisms, as I mentioned earlier, come in two varieties—*criticisms of arguments* and *criticisms of positions*. A successful criticism of an argument points out how the argument fails to provide a reason for thinking the position is true, because the argument fails to meet the requirements of a cogent argument, viz., the argument

20

either 1) has premises that are no more reasonable to believe than its conclusion or 2) fails to reliably make its conclusion even probably true. A successful criticism of a position, on the other hand, points out a reason to believe the position is false.

One of the most popular, effective, and fun ways of criticizing someone's position is to illustrate how that position has further implications that are patently false; that is to say, the position is incompatible with obvious facts. This form of criticism is called *reductio ad absurdum*—literally translated: reduced to the absurd.

Here's an example. Take as our target, the position that animals have rights similar to those of human beings, by virtue of their being sentient (i.e., able to experience, for example, pain). If animals have similar rights to life and liberty, however, this would imply that those who raise livestock are on a moral par with slave owners and mass murderers. And this would, in turn, imply that they should be treated as such—at least incarcerated for life for their crimes. But this is patently absurd!

Our opponent now has three options. 1) Maintain their position, but reject the new implication—but in doing this, they would be guilty of an inconsistency. 2) Remain consistent, bite the bullet, and adopt the new implication of their original position—but in doing this, they are adopting a position that is obviously false. 3) Reject what is forcing them between the rock of 1) and the hard place of 2); namely, reject their original position—but in doing this, the critic has won the day.

Your strategy, when giving a *reductio*, is to find an *implication* of your targeted alternative position—an implication that is *patently absurd*. In this way you leave your opponent with only the third option, which is with-drawing their position.

You can also use a *reductio* to criticize an argument. Just illustrate how your opponent's argument not only supports the conclusion or position they hold dear, but also equally well supports another conclusion—one that is patently false or absurd. For example, the *reductio* given above could be used against someone who has argued that abortion after ten weeks into the pregnancy is immoral because the fetus has the right to life by virtue of its sentience. The sentience argument for fetal rights would equally well support the conclusion that animals have the right to life, and, well, now you know the rest of the story!

Always remember, however, that a *reductio* against an opponent's *argument*, if successful, is only a reason for rejecting the argument; it's *not* a reason for thinking the opponent's position is false.


### *Beware of begging the question*

When you are critically reviewing alternative positions, it is very tempting and easy to argue against those positions by simply assuming the truth of your own position and then faulting them for being incompatible with yours. To argue this way is to commit the fallacy of begging the question. Consider the following example.

Say you have taken the position that state-enforced welfare policies are morally justified, and say you have argued for this position by arguing for the right of the needy to assis-tance when it is at minimal cost to others. As an alternative position, you then cite the Libertarian position against welfare, which argues that the State's method of financing the welfare system through taxation is simply legalized robbery—taking money from people without their consent. Now, what if you made the following reply? "The Libertarian's charges of robbery simply can't stick, because one can't rob someone of money one has a right to get in the first place, and the needy have a right to the money —the State is just seeing to it that the needy's rights to it are protected."

Something is extremely fishy about this reply—it merely assumes (your original position) that the needy have a right to assistance and then concludes that the Libertarian argument is wrong to imply otherwise. You can now see why begging the question is such an ineffective form of criticism: It's in essence just to say to your opponent, "You're wrong because I'm right." But, of course, your opponent could then say the same thing right back to you!

The best way to avoid begging the question, as you argue against your opponents' positions and arguments, is to formulate criticisms that are completely independent of any position on the issue you're discussing. Imagine that you have no position whatsoever on the issue. Such a critic can't possibly beg the question, because they have no position to beg, while they are critically reviewing the alternatives.

### Beware of straw men

As you are criticizing an opponent's position, make sure you really *are* criticizing that position, as opposed to a more easily criticized misrepresentation of the position—a straw man. (This same point holds as you are criticizing *arguments* too.)

An example will help you to understand this fallacy. In an article on abortion, Mary Ann Warren defends the position that in order to be a person and, in turn, a rightsholder, one must have various cognitive capacities such as consciousness and reasoning. In response, John Noonan launches the *reductio* criticism that Warren's position would imply that someone who had passed out would lose their status as a person and, therefore, lose their rights. But, do you see the straw man here? Warren's position concerned the *capacities* of consciousness and reasoning—even though someone who has passed out has lost consciousness and is currently not doing any reasoning, they still have both *capacities*. So this criticism fails to address Warren's position and instead hits only a straw man misrepresentation of that position.

To ensure that you have not misrepresented your targeted alternative position (or its argument), supply evidence for your reconstruction of it. This is one time when ample quotations to support your reconstruction may be helpful.

### A question is never a criticism

Quite often, an author of a position does not anticipate all possible questions, the answers to which might clarify and complete their position. This failure, however, does not constitute a criticism, because it's always open to the author to answer such questions in a reasonable fashion. So, just raising unanswered questions gives no reason whatsoever for thinking the position to which those questions are directed is false.

An example will clarify this. In the famous Supreme Court decision *Roe v. Wade,* the Court defended the position that the fetus acquires moral status at viability. The Court

24

defines viability as the point at which the fetus would survive if it were removed from the womb and given artificial aid. A common criticism made against this position is the question, "How much artificial aid?" The Court simply failed to explicitly answer this question and specify how much. But if one treats this question as a criticism, it could quickly be met by the Court. All the Court needs to do is non-arbitrarily and explicitly specify how much artificial aid. And it can do that quite easily: State-of-the-art medical technology. The question is thereby answered; the criticism is thereby met.

Another popular, but no less erroneous, way of trying to make a question into a criticism is to ask, "Who's to say?"; for example, "Who's to say when we acquire moral status?" But this is the easiest criticism of all to meet. The Court, for example, can simply reply, "*We* are to say, for the reasons we just gave; weren't you reading closely, Bozo?"

*Never* say, "Who's to say?" because, of course, the answer is obvious: The person with the best arguments and the fewest criticisms is the one "Who is to say"!

The only time it's appropriate to say "Who is to say?' is if the issue is just a subjective matter of taste. But then, of course, one must also *argue* that it is!


## How the second half of your paper looks

From a bird's eye view, the critical review portion of your paper looks something like this:

1. Reconstruction of alternative position #1
2. Reconstruction of argument for that alternative position
3. Criticism of that argument
4. Criticism of alternative position #1
5. Reconstruction of alternative position #2
6. Reconstruction of argument for that alternative position
7. Criticism of that argument
8. Criticism of alternative position #2

Stick pretty closely to the order of things detailed above. Don't rattle off all your reconstructions of alternative positions and then all their arguments and then all your criticisms. This would invariably lead to confusion, as you force your reader to flip pages, trying to match up your criticisms with their targeted arguments and positions.

If you have only one alternative position in competition with yours, you obviously need only go through steps 1-4. But you may, then, wish to supply more criticisms of your opponent's arguments and position, repeating steps 1-4, for a more thorough critical review of your only competition.

## An alternative approach to assembling your paper

Often, it's easier and more efficient to organize your paper *in reverse*. You begin, as usual, with a clear statement of your position and (if necessary) an introductory preface as to the relevance of the issue you're addressing. But rather than launching into your arguments for your position, it might be better to critically review alternative positions first.

This is especially true when your position is an amended version of an alternative position or when aspects or virtues of your position are more easily understood and appreciated after looking at the problems with alternative positions. Various planks in your position might have been chosen by you so as to solve the problems with alternative positions. So it might well be the case that you would aid the reader by first "clearing away dead wood" with a critical review of your opponents.

Another reason to critically review alternative positions first is that it often results in a more effective, persuasive paper, when your audience is a bit locked into their own position already. As well as you may present a case for your position, this kind of audience is disposed to think, "Well, I've got my position, and I've got arguments for it too, so There." But if you first wipe out their reasons for thinking their position is true and then actually give them reasons for thinking their position is false, they are going to be much more receptive to your position, after you've left them in desperate need of a new one.

You have to be the judge of the more effective way of assembling your position paper. The thing to remember, however, is that no matter which way you select, all the basic ingredients must be included.

The danger with using this reverse approach is forgetting to include arguments for your position and ending up with only a critical review of alternative positions, prefaced by a mere assertion of your own. This can never pass as a position paper; no number of successful criticisms of alternative positions can function as even a *single* reason for believing yours.

**The closing paragraph**

There are at least three popular ways of ending a position paper. You must be the judge as to which way works best for the particular paper you're writing. You might even incorporate all three of the following approaches.

One option is to provide a very brief summary of your paper; for example, "In this paper I defended the position that... and argued for its greater defensibility in comparison to the alternative positions which state that...."

The only thing to beware of, when closing your paper this way, is that your summary can easily appear redundant, especially if your paper is short. But a summarizing closing paragraph is still very helpful to the reader who didn't follow your paper well enough. It provides them with a checklist to confirm that they understood your paper.

BTW: This kind of summary paragraph might be useful to your readers at various times throughout your paper, to use as a checklist to confirm that they have followed your discussions.

Another option is to point out the broadening scope of your position and arguments by discussing their implications with respect to *other* issues. For example, after having defended the Minnesota Supreme Court's decision (in *RAV v. St. Paul*) to prohibit additional sentencing for "hate crimes" (crimes motivated by bigotry), you could close by discussing how that defense would also support the prohibition of campus "hate speech" codes, such as the one abandoned at the University of Wisconsin-Madison.

Yet another option is to discuss how your position is to be implemented. What do you think ought to be done, given that your position is true?  For example, say you defended the position that George Bush used racist ads during the 1988 presidential campaign.  You might then suggest steps that could be taken to deter such practices in future political campaigns, for instance, having candidates voluntarily submit their ads to organizations of groups that might find them derogatory (just as Jay Leno does with his jokes).

No matter which approaches you adopt when writing your closing paragraph, you want to end your paper conveying the impression that you have covered the basic ingredients of a position paper.


## The process of writing your position paper

Here are all the elements of a position paper we've discussed.

1. Introductory statement
2. Statement of position
3. Argument for position
4. Reconstruction of criticism of argument for position
5. Criticism of criticism of argument for position
6. Reconstruction of criticism of position
7. Criticism of criticism of position
8. Reconstruction of alternative position
9. Reconstruction of argument for alternative position
10. Criticism of argument for alternative position
11. Criticism of alternative position
12. Closing paragraph

Don't think for a minute, however, that this outline lists the order in which you must *create* your paper.  Virtually all these basic ingredients must appear in the final draft of your paper, but in what order you write them is up to you and can vary from paper to paper.

Begin where it's most comfortable and decide later how to organize your paper—whether you want to argue for your position before or after critically reviewing alternative positions. My advice is to write each element of your paper on a separate page. Then, after you have all the elements individually printed out, lay them out on the floor and read over them, to see which is the most effective approach to take—position defended first or critical review presented first.

Another benefit of this building-block approach to composing your paper is that you can begin to write your position paper without first having a position. If you don't know what position to take on an issue, you know at least this much: *You should adopt the position that has the best arguments and the fewest criticisms.* That is the *rational* position to adopt.

So use the process of writing as a way of discovering which position is most rational to adopt: *On separate sheets of paper*, reconstruct the various positions you are aware of and reconstruct their respective arguments, along with the respective criticisms of these arguments and of these positions. After doing all this reconstructing, lay all your pages out on the floor, step back, and note the relations among these positions, arguments, and criticisms. The figure on the next page typifies the dynamic map of positions, arguments, and criticisms you will create.

After a thorough survey of all these pieces of the debate, ask yourself, "OK, who's faring best here?" Whichever position that is, you ought to adopt and defend it in your position paper. Your paper is essentially written at this point. All you need to do is write a clear statement of commitment to the position you have discovered to be the winner, organize your pages, and properly flag each element on each page.

This building-block approach helps you discover what positions you ought to adopt. It also helps keep you from habitually or ignorantly digging in your heels on a position, when you come to realize that yours is not the position with the best arguments and the fewest criticisms.

*In fact, this approach to composing a position paper is what critical thinking is all about!*

**Pop Quiz:** Here's what your floor might look like as you think about which position to adopt: Which of the three positions laid out below would be the most rational to defend?

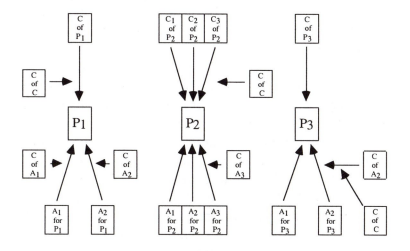

The answer is P3. Can you explain why?

If, after writing your paper, you discover that it would be more rational to adopt an *alternative* position, *don't throw your paper away!* Just take out a scissors and cut your paper into the basic elements that we've been discussing all this time. What *was* your position now becomes a worthy opponent, and the criticisms of what was your position (or its arguments) become criticisms of an alternative position (or its arguments). And what was your most worthy opponent, now becomes your position, after you found that it was the one with the best arguments and the fewest criticisms. Just reorganize your pieces and reflag them.


**Citing your sources**

One of the questions most frequently asked by students is, "Do I have to come up with my own position and arguments, or can I use other people's?" The answer is, of course you can adopt other people's positions and use other people's arguments. Publishing would be absurdly self-defeating if making a position or argument public made it off limits for others to adopt.

All you are required to do, when you adopt another's position, argument, or criticism is to give credit where credit is due. Attribute it to its author. Cite your source, either formally in a footnote or at least informally in the body of your paper; for example, "My first argument is Peter Singer's, from 'All Animals are Equal'." Ask your instructor which format they prefer. Failing to cite your sources is plagiarism, among the worst of the intellectual dishonesties. If the source for your position, argument, or criticism is your instructor, they too must be cited as discussed above.

The benefit of citing your sources, besides that of avoiding the charge of plagiarism, is that it helps your audience give you a charitable reading. Say you use someone else's argument to support your position, but you've given such a clumsy or ambiguous rendition of that argument that your reader can't quite figure out what you're saying. If you would have said that it was so-and-so's argument, however, the reader might have been able to give you the benefit of the doubt, thinking, "Oh, *now* I see what she's driving at; she just stated the argument poorly." Now you're merely guilty of bad writing, instead of the stronger charge of hurling nonsense.

When you use other peoples' positions, arguments, or criticisms, don't just quote or parrot them. Put their positions, arguments, or criticisms in your own words, avoiding or at least defining any jargon or buzzwords used by the authors. Putting things in your own non-technical words will not only facilitate your reader's understanding, it will also show your reader that *you* understand what you're talking about.

Another helpful thing you can do for your reader is to use examples. For instance, if you have taken the position against the general use of animal experiments, give some specific examples in which you think the use of lab animals was particularly morally objectionable. Such examples, however, are just for purposes of illustrating and clarifying your position. They do *not* constitute *arguments* for your position. To use them as arguments is just to beg the question.

If you have an *original* position, argument, or criticism, and you want to use it in your paper, that's fantastic! I'm the first to encourage such original thinking. But expect to have your position, argument, or criticism critically reviewed by your reader as thoroughly as any other author's. *Creative thinking is not necessarily critical thinking.* So while there is plenty of room for original thinking in your position paper, a position, argument, or criticism is no better just because *you* happened to have thought of it. But even after these rather gloomy words, remember this: You learn as much from your errors as you do from your successes, in a position paper.

## Writing style

The writing style used in this writing guide is rather informal and conversational. I use a lot of contractions, for example, and words like 'a lot.' I even use technically incorrect grammar; for example, I should have said that I "use words *such as* 'a lot'." But I do this for a reason: I want to lay out in ordinary, easy, friendly language what it is to produce a good position paper.

Don't get me wrong. Word choice is crucial, but it's crucial primarily for conveying the contents of your paper. Differences in positions can hinge on a single word. Effectiveness of an argument can hinge on a single word. But nothing hinges on your saying "I *will* defend the position that..." or "I *shall* defend the position that...," although the latter is *technically* correct, grammatically. Don't get me wrong here either. I'm not saying that rules of grammar have faded away. I'm just saying that recently some rules of grammar have become more flexible, so as to become more user friendly.

Position papers, by virtue of the basic ingredients they must contain, are going to be more formal than, for example, personal journals or letters. But position papers need not be stuffy. You must decide how informal or conversational you may get by keeping an eye on your audience, especially the person ultimately assessing the paper. To some instructors, a more conversational style of writing is distracting, like loud music playing while one is trying to read.

Other concerns you should keep in mind are misspellings and typos on your final draft. Many instructors view them as indicators of how much you care about the paper assignment: If you didn't care enough to proof the paper, then you didn't care enough to write a thoughtful one. These instructors have probability on their side! And even if you are the exception to the rule, don't expect to be a *noted* exception. Just take a few minutes, run your spelling check, and proof your paper thoroughly before you hit the print button for the last time.

### Nonsexist language

Another consideration with respect to writing style and word choice is the use of nonsexist or non-exclusionary language. A sure way to alienate your reader is to omit them from the discussion of an issue when that issue applies equally to them. And you will be interpreted as doing exactly that when you talk of "man" and "mankind" and use only male pronouns; for example, 'he' and 'his,' when referring to people. When you stake out a position about "what *man* ought to do for his fellow *man*," you leave out 51% of the population. To claim that 'man' is gender neutral, meaning simply people, is as lame as claiming that 'coloreds' is racially neutral, that it simply means African Americans. Given the history of these terms, they just aren't neutral no matter how much the person who uses them intends that they are. These terms are demeaning to a major audience, so don't use them—just consider it a courtesy to the reader.

Rather than 'man' or 'mankind,' use 'persons' or 'people.' Rather than using 'he' all the time to refer to people generally, alternate it with 'she' or replace it with 's/he.' Or replace 'he' with 'one,' 'anyone,' or 'everyone,' depending on the level of formality in your writing style. You could also use plural forms of nouns and avoid the problem; for example, rather than saying, "The student is responsible for any damages to his room," say "Students are responsible for any damages to their rooms." Another option is to use 'he or she,' 'him or her,' 'his or hers,' and 'himself or herself,' but this is cumbersome and distracting for some readers [me, for one].

Recently, it has become perfectly acceptable to use plural pronouns for singular reference. So, the example above would become, "The student is responsible for any damages to their room." You might have noticed that *I* have been using plural pronouns in this way all this time. [If you *didn't* notice that I was doing this, take it as evidence for the reader friendliness of this practice.] Not everyone is familiar with the acceptability of this practice. And, as a student, you belong to a group that is not exactly well known for its grammatical proficiencies. [No offense intended!] So, if you decide to adopt this practice in your paper, you might consider including a parenthetical remark or a footnote to the reader right from the start; for example, "Throughout this paper, I use plural pronouns for singular reference." Telling the reader this, might well save you from their charge of using nonparallel constructions. [See? I did it again, and it sounded fine.]

## Help

The best source of help with writing your position paper is, of course, your instructor who assigned it. But don't expect them to read rough drafts. This would significantly multiply their grading time, which is likely to be excessive already. During their office hours, however, there should be time to check *an outline* of your paper, to see if you've included all the basic elements and to verify that you haven't used arguments that are on record as having problems.

Another source of help is your school's writing lab. Talking your paper through with someone at the writing lab will help you find the gaps in your paper and some alternative ways of wording things. Writing lab assistants are especially good at helping people bridge the chasm between conversing about an issue and defending a position on it. They can also help you with matters of grammar, punctuation, and writing style.

## Where to find position papers

You are actually surrounded by position papers—that's why it's so important to know how to read and write them. But if you're looking for some good examples to practice dissecting and analyzing, here are some suggestions.

For short position papers, take a look at your student or local newspaper's opinion page—the letters to the editor and the editorials. Some great letters and editorials can be found in major newspapers, such as *The New York Times, The L.A. Times, The Washington Post*, and many others.

Political commentary magazines, such as *The New Republic*, consist largely of position papers and critical reviews. And you don't even have to subscribe to them. Just check their Web sites for complete articles.

A vast Web collection of position papers and critical reviews [and much, much more] is found in LEXIS-NEXIS. It can be accessed through most university library Web sites and allows you to do searches on topics discussed in the top 50 newspapers and hundreds of periodicals and journals.

Philosophy is a great source of position papers, especially ethics. For a sample of Web links to these resources, you are welcome to check the philosophy department's Web site at Winona State University: http://www.winona.edu.

While your library will always have a wealth of position papers for you, the Web really has become a wonderful, often credible source. For example, try the search engine Google. Click on its Directory link and then click the Society Issues link. If the topic that interests you is not in the initial list, look under the more complete alphabet listing. You'll find the Web sites of many reputable research groups, organizations, and think tanks, with hundreds of posted articles.

For a substantial collection of papers nicely organized in debate style, see http://www.nationalissues.com.

Enjoy!

## Conclusion

I hope that this writing manual helps you not only to write better position papers, but also helps you make some discoveries, about yourself and the world of ideas.

I close with a checklist concerning the elements of a position paper, for your easy reference. Immediately following each listed element of a position paper is a question [or a "heuristic," as the folks in composition theory would called them]. When you are performing the "anatomy of a position paper," identifying all its parts, you can use these questions: Ask the question, find the answer in the paper, and you've found the part! Also ask these questions of *yourself*, as you are writing your position paper, so that you can verify that your paper is complete.

Also included is a famous example of a position paper, with its parts identified immediately after. [See if you agree with my answers.] It's Jonathan Swift's satirical article, "A Modest Proposal." Swift disobeys the rule about kicking things off with one's statement of position. When you do the anatomy of the article, you'll see why. You will also see how artful one must be to keep the reader's attention when this writing style is used.

*Good luck on your papers!*

# CHECKLIST

## Elements of a Position Paper—Repeat as Needed

1. Introductory statement as to the relevance of the issue. Why should anyone give a damn about this issue?

2. Statement of position. What is my position on this issue?

3. Argument for position. What is my main reason for thinking my position is correct?

4. Reconstruction of criticisms of that argument. Are there any criticisms of my argument? If so, what are they?

5. Criticisms of criticisms of that argument. Are there any criticisms of these criticisms? If so, what are they? If not, find a better argument!

6. Reconstruction of criticisms of position. Are there any reasons for thinking my position is false? If so, what are they?

7. Criticisms of criticism of position. Are there any criticisms of these criticisms? If so, what are they? If not, find a better position!

8. Reconstruction of alternative position. What is my most worthy or popular opponent on this issue?

9. Reconstruction of argument for alternative position. What is the best reason for thinking this alternative position is correct?

10. Criticism of that argument. Why doesn't that argument successfully support the alternative position?

11. Criticism of alternative position. What reasons are there for thinking the alternative position is false?

12. Closing paragraph.

# Reminders

- Avoid fluffy introductions.

- Use paragraph breaks for each element of your paper.

- Properly "flag" each element of your paper.

- Keep your audience in mind to determine your fundamental assumptions.

- Write your paper for the non-expert.

- Avoid jargon and quotations—put things in your own words.

- Cite your sources—give credit where it's due.

- Keep your audience in mind to determine what writing style to adopt.

- Avoid sexist language.

- Proof read your paper for typos, misspellings, and grammatical errors.

# A Modest Proposal
## For Preventing The Children of Poor People in Ireland From Being a Burden to Their Parents or Country, and For Making Them Beneficial to The Public

### Jonathan Swift

1. It is a melancholy object to those who walk through this great town or travel in the country, when they see the streets, the roads, and cabin doors, crowded with beggars of the female sex, followed by three, four, or six children, all in rags and importuning every passenger for an alms. These mothers, instead of being able to work for their honest livelihood, are forced to employ all their time in strolling to beg sustenance for their helpless infants: who as they grow up either turn thieves for want of work, or leave their dear native country to fight for the Pretender in Spain, or sell themselves to the Barbadoes.

2. I think it is agreed by all parties that this prodigious number of children in the arms, or on the backs, or at the heels of their mothers, and frequently of their fathers, is in the present deplorable state of the kingdom a very great additional grievance; and, therefore, whoever could find out a fair, cheap, and easy method of making these children sound, useful members of the commonwealth, would deserve so well of the public as to have his statue set up for a preserver of the nation.

3. But my intention is very far from being confined to provide only for the children of professed beggars; it is of a much greater extent, and shall take in the whole number of infants at a certain age who are born of parents in effect as little able to support them as those who demand our charity in the streets.

4. As to my own part, having turned my thoughts for many years upon this important subject, and maturely weighed the several schemes of other projectors, I have always found them grossly mistaken in the computation. It is true, a child just dropped from its dam may be supported by her milk for a solar year, with little other nourishment; at most not above the value of 2s., which the mother may certainly get, or the value in scraps, by her lawful occupation of begging; and it is exactly at one year old that I propose to provide for them in such a manner as instead of being a charge upon their parents or the parish, or wanting food and raiment for the rest of their lives, they shall on the contrary contribute to the feeding, and partly to the clothing, of many thousands.

5. There is likewise another great advantage in my scheme, that it will prevent those voluntary abortions, and that horrid practice of women murdering their bastard children, alas! too frequent among us! sacrificing the poor innocent babes I doubt more to avoid the expense than the shame, which would move tears and pity in the most savage and inhuman breast.

6. The number of souls in this kingdom being usually reckoned one million and a half, of these I calculate there may be about two hundred thousand couple whose wives are breeders; from which number I subtract thirty thousand couples who are able to maintain their own children, although I apprehend there cannot be so many, under the present distresses of the kingdom; but this being granted, there will remain an hundred and seventy thousand breeders. I again subtract fifty thousand for those women who miscarry, or whose children die by accident or disease within the year.

There only remains one hundred and twenty thousand children of poor parents annually born. The question therefore is, how this number shall be reared and provided for, which, as I have already said, under the present situation of affairs, is utterly impossible by all the methods hitherto proposed. For we can neither employ them in handicraft or agriculture; we neither build houses (I mean in the country) nor cultivate land: they can very seldom pick up a livelihood by stealing, till they arrive at six years old, except where they are of towardly parts, although I confess they learn the rudiments much earlier, during which time, they can however be properly looked upon only as probationers, as I have been informed by a principal gentleman in the county of Cavan, who protested to me that he never knew above one or two instances under the age of six, even in a part of the kingdom so renowned for the quickest proficiency in that art.

7. I am assured by our merchants, that a boy or a girl before twelve years old is no salable commodity; and even when they come to this age they will not yield above three pounds, or three pounds and half-a-crown at most on the exchange; which cannot turn to account either to the parents or kingdom, the charge of nutriment and rags having been at least four times that value.

8. I shall now therefore humbly propose my own thoughts, which I hope will not be liable to the least objection.

9. I have been assured by a very knowing American of my acquaintance in London, that a young healthy child well nursed is at a year old a most delicious, nourishing, and wholesome food, whether stewed, roasted, baked, or

boiled; and I make no doubt that it will equally serve in a fricassee or a ragout.

10. I do therefore humbly offer it to public consideration that of the hundred and twenty thousand children already computed, twenty thousand may be reserved for breed, whereof only one-fourth part to be males; which is more than we allow to sheep, black cattle or swine; and my reason is, that these children are seldom the fruits of marriage, a circumstance not much regarded by our savages, therefore one male will be sufficient to serve four females. That the remaining hundred thousand may, at a year old, be offered in the sale to the persons of quality and fortune through the kingdom; always advising the mother to let them suck plentifully in the last month, so as to render them plump and fat for a good table. A child will make two dishes at an entertainment for friends; and when the family dines alone, the fore or hind quarter will make a reasonable dish, and seasoned with a little pepper or salt will be very good boiled on the fourth day, especially in winter.

11. I have reckoned upon a medium that a child just born will weigh 12 pounds, and in a solar year, if tolerably nursed, increaseth to 28 pounds.

12. I grant this food will be somewhat dear, and therefore very proper for landlords, who, as they have already devoured most of the parents, seem to have the best title to the children.

13. Infant's flesh will be in season throughout the year, but more plentiful in March, and a little before and after; for we are told by a grave author, an eminent French physician, that fish being a prolific diet, there are more children born in Roman Catholic countries about nine

months after Lent than at any other season; therefore, reckoning a year after Lent, the markets will be more glutted than usual, because the number of popish infants is at least three to one in this kingdom: and therefore it will have one other collateral advantage, by lessening the number of papists among us.

14. I have already computed the charge of nursing a beggar's child (in which list I reckon all cottagers, laborers, and four-fifths of the farmers) to be about two shillings per annum, rags included; and I believe no gentleman would repine to give ten shillings for the carcass of a good fat child, which, as I have said, will make four dishes of excellent nutritive meat, when he hath only some particular friend or his own family to dine with him. Thus the squire will learn to be a good landlord, and grow popular among his tenants; the mother will have eight shillings net profit, and be fit for work till she produces another child.

15. Those who are more thrifty (as I must confess the times require) may flay the carcass; the skin of which artificially dressed will make admirable gloves for ladies, and summer boots for fine gentlemen.

16. As to our city of Dublin, shambles may be appointed for this purpose in the most convenient parts of it, and butchers we may be assured will not be wanting; although I rather recommend buying the children alive, and dressing them hot from the knife, as we do roasting pigs.

17. A very worthy person, a true lover of his country, and whose virtues I highly esteem, was lately pleased in discoursing on this matter to offer a refinement upon my scheme. He said that many gentlemen of this

kingdom, having of late destroyed their deer, he conceived that the want of venison might be well supplied by the bodies of young lads and maidens, not exceeding fourteen years of age nor under twelve; so great a number of both sexes in every country being now ready to starve for want of work and service; and these to be disposed of by their parents, if alive, or otherwise by their nearest relations. But with due deference to so excellent a friend and so deserving a patriot, I cannot be altogether in his sentiments; for as to the males, my American acquaintance assured me, from frequent experience, that their flesh was generally tough and lean, like that of our schoolboys by continual exercise, and their taste disagreeable; and to fatten them would not answer the charge. Then as to the females, it would, I think, with humble submission be a loss to the public, because they soon would become breeders themselves; and besides, it is not improbable that some scrupulous people might be apt to censure such a practice (although indeed very unjustly), as a little bordering upon cruelty; which, I confess, hath always been with me the strongest objection against any project, however so well intended.

18. But in order to justify my friend, he confessed that this expedient was put into his head by the famous Psalmanazar, a native of the island Formosa, who came from thence to London above twenty years ago, and in conversation told my friend, that in his country when any young person happened to be put to death, the executioner sold the carcass to persons of quality as a prime dainty; and that in his time the body of a plump girl of fifteen, who was crucified for an attempt to poison the emperor, was sold to his imperial majesty's prime minister of state, and other great mandarins of the court, in joints from the gibbet, at four hundred crowns.

Neither indeed can I deny, that if the same use were made of several plump young girls in this town, who without one single groat to their fortunes cannot stir abroad without a chair, and appear at playhouse and assemblies in foreign fineries which they never will pay for, the kingdom would not be the worse.

19. Some persons of a desponding spirit are in great concern about that vast number of poor people, who are aged, diseased, or maimed, and I have been desired to employ my thoughts what course may be taken to ease the nation of so grievous an encumbrance. But I am not in the least pain upon that matter, because it is very well known that they are every day dying and rotting by cold and famine, and filth and vermin, as fast as can be reasonably expected. And as to the young laborers, they are now in as hopeful a condition; they cannot get work, and consequently pine away for want of nourishment, to a degree that if at any time they are accidentally hired to common labor, they have not strength to perform it; and thus the country and themselves are happily delivered from the evils to come.

20. I have too long digressed, and therefore shall return to my subject. I think the advantages by the proposal which I have made are obvious and many, as well as of the highest importance.

21. For first, as I have already observed, it would greatly lessen the number of papists, with whom we are yearly overrun, being the principal breeders of the nation as well as our most dangerous enemies; and who stay at home on purpose with a design to deliver the kingdom to the Pretender, hoping to take their advantage by the absence of so many good protestants, who have chosen

rather to leave their country than stay at home and pay tithes against their conscience to an episcopal curate.

22. Secondly, The poorer tenants will have something valuable of their own, which by law may be made liable to distress and help to pay their landlord's rent, their corn and cattle being already seized, and money a thing unknown.

23. Thirdly, Whereas the maintenance of an hundred thousand children, from two years old and upward, cannot be computed at less than ten shillings a-piece per annum, the nation's stock will be thereby increased fifty thousand pounds per annum, beside the profit of a new dish introduced to the tables of all gentlemen of fortune in the kingdom who have any refinement in taste. And the money will circulate among ourselves, the goods being entirely of our own growth and manufacture.

24. Fourthly, The constant breeders, beside the gain of eight shillings sterling per annum by the sale of their children, will be rid of the charge of maintaining them after the first year.

25. Fifthly, This food would likewise bring great custom to taverns; where the vintners will certainly be so prudent as to procure the best receipts for dressing it to perfection, and consequently have their houses frequented by all the fine gentlemen, who justly value themselves upon their knowledge in good eating: and a skilful cook, who understands how to oblige his guests, will contrive to make it as expensive as they please.

26. Sixthly, This would be a great inducement to marriage, which all wise nations have either encouraged by

rewards or enforced by laws and penalties. It would increase the care and tenderness of mothers toward their children, when they were sure of a settlement for life to the poor babes, provided in some sort by the public, to their annual profit instead of expense. We should see an honest emulation among the married women, which of them could bring the fattest child to the market. Men would become as fond of their wives during the time of their pregnancy as they are now of their mares in foal, their cows in calf, their sows when they are ready to farrow; nor offer to beat or kick them (as is too frequent a practice) for fear of a miscarriage.

27. Many other advantages might be enumerated. For instance, the addition of some thousand carcasses in our exportation of barreled beef, the propagation of swine's flesh, and improvement in the art of making good bacon, so much wanted among us by the great destruction of pigs, too frequent at our tables; which are no way comparable in taste or magnificence to a well-grown, fat, yearling child, which roasted whole will make a considerable figure at a lord mayor's feast or any other public entertainment. But this and many others I omit, being studious of brevity.

28. Supposing that one thousand families in this city would be constant customers for infants' flesh, besides others who might have it at merry meetings, particularly weddings and christenings, I compute that Dublin would take off annually about twenty thousand carcasses, and the rest of the kingdom (where probably they will be sold somewhat cheaper) the remaining eighty thousand.

29. I can think of no one objection that will possibly be raised against this proposal, unless it should be urged

that the number of people will be thereby much lessened in the kingdom. This I freely own, and it was indeed one principal design in offering it to the world. I desire the reader will observe, that I calculate my remedy for this one individual kingdom of Ireland and for no other that ever was, is, or I think ever can be upon earth. Therefore let no man talk to me of other expedients: of taxing our absentees at five shillings a pound: of using neither clothes nor household furniture except what is of our own growth and manufacture: of utterly rejecting the materials and instruments that promote foreign luxury: of curing the expensiveness of pride, vanity, idleness, and gaming in our women: of introducing a vein of parsimony, prudence, and temperance: of learning to love our country, in the want of which we differ even from Laplanders and the inhabitants of Topinamboo: of quitting our animosities and factions, nor acting any longer like the Jews, who were murdering one another at the very moment their city was taken: of being a little cautious not to sell our country and conscience for nothing: of teaching landlords to have at least one degree of mercy toward their tenants: lastly, of putting a spirit of honesty, industry, and skill into our shopkeepers; who, if a resolution could now be taken to buy only our native goods, would immediately unite to cheat and exact upon us in the price, the measure, and the goodness, nor could ever yet be brought to make one fair proposal of just dealing, though often and earnestly invited to it.

30. Therefore I repeat, let no man talk to me of these and the like expedients, till he hath at least some glimpse of hope that there will ever be some hearty and sincere attempt to put them in practice.

31. But as to myself, having been wearied out for many years with offering vain, idle, visionary thoughts, and at length utterly despairing of success, I fortunately fell upon this proposal, which, as it is wholly new, so it hath something solid and real, of no expense and little trouble, full in our own power, and whereby we can incur no danger in disobliging England. For this kind of commodity will not bear exportation, the flesh being of too tender a consistence to admit a long continuance in salt, although perhaps I could name a country which would be glad to eat up our whole nation without it.

32. After all, I am not so violently bent upon my own opinion as to reject any offer proposed by wise men, which shall be found equally innocent, cheap, easy, and effectual. But before something of that kind shall be advanced in contradiction to my scheme, and offering a better, I desire the author or authors will be pleased maturely to consider two points. First, as things now stand, how they will be able to find food and raiment for an hundred thousand useless mouths and backs. And secondly, there being a round million of creatures in human figure throughout this kingdom, whose whole subsistence put into a common stock would leave them in debt two millions of pounds sterling, adding those who are beggars by profession to the bulk of farmers, cottagers, and laborers, with their wives and children who are beggars in effect: I desire those politicians who dislike my overture, and may perhaps be so bold as to attempt an answer, that they will first ask the parents of these mortals, whether they would not at this day think it a great happiness to have been sold for food, at a year old in the manner I prescribe, and thereby have avoided such a perpetual scene of misfortunes as they have since gone through by the oppression of landlords, the impossibility of paying rent without money or trade, the

want of common sustenance, with neither house nor clothes to cover them from the inclemencies of the weather, and the most inevitable prospect of entailing the like or greater miseries upon their breed for ever.

33. I profess, in the sincerity of my heart, that I have not the least personal interest in endeavoring to promote this necessary work, having no other motive than the public good of my country, by advancing our trade, providing for infants, relieving the poor, and giving some pleasure to the rich. I have no children by which I can propose to get a single penny; the youngest being nine years old, and my wife past child-bearing.

# Anatomy of *A Modest Proposal*

1. Intro.
2. Intro.
3. Intro.
4. Argument for Position
5. Arg. for Position
6. Criticism of Alternative Position
7. Crit. of Alt. Position
8. Nothing / flag of Position
9. Arg. for Position
10. Position
11. Position
12. Position and Arg. for Position
13. Arg. for Position
14. Arg. for Position
15. Arg. for Position
16. Arg. for Position / Position
17. Alt. Position and Crit. of Alt. Position
18. Position
19. Position and Arg. for Position
20. Nothing / flag of Arguments
21. Arg. for Position
22. Arg. for Position
23. Arg. for Position
24. Arg. for Position
25. Arg. for Position
26. Arg. for Position
27. Arg. for Position
28. Position
29. Crit. of Position, Crit. of Crit. of Position, Alt. Position, and Crit. of Alt. Position
30. Crit. of Alt. Position
31. Arg. for Position
32. Arg. for Position
33. Closing Paragraph